Contents

Any words appearing in the text in bold,
like this, are explained in the Glossary.

Introduction

In the last 60 years or so, advances in weapons technology have led to huge changes in the nature of warfare. In July 1943, during World War II, UK and US air forces tried to damage the German war effort with huge bombing raids on the port of Hamburg. The air forces dropped thousands of tonnes of bombs, land mines and incendiaries (fire bombs). The city was all but destroyed, over 40,000 people were killed, and many more were wounded or made homeless. But these massive raids could not knock Germany out of the war, and German industry soon recovered.

By the time of the 1991 Gulf War, things were very different. In this war the USA and a **coalition** of other countries went to war against Iraq when it invaded Kuwait. The coalition forces used hi-tech weapons to reduce the Iraqis' ability to wage war, rather than killing thousands of soldiers and civilians. First, precision missiles were used to attack the command system of the Iraqi government and its armed forces. The missiles could destroy targets with great accuracy, even targets in cities. Each one was as effective as hundreds of World War II bombs. The Iraqi forces were weakened without coalition soldiers having to risk their lives, and with much less loss to civilian life. By the time coalition ground troops were sent in, much of the Iraqi army had already been defeated.

Warfare today

The 1991 Gulf War was a **conventional war**, in which two opposing armies fought each other using large numbers of soldiers, tanks, armoured vehicles and aircraft. But today, armed forces are increasingly involved in other kinds of conflict, such as **guerrilla** war and **terrorism**. Modern armies are not equipped to deal with an enemy that does not engage in any form of 'battle'. For these kinds of warfare a different kind of fighting force, using different tactics, is needed.

Guerrillas are small groups of irregular soldiers who fight against a much bigger occupying army. They often have the support of the local population. Terrorist groups usually have political aims. As their name suggests, they

The machinery of conventional warfare. Huge convoys of military vehicles moved into Iraq at the start of the Iraq war in 2003.

try to create terror and fear, for instance through **hijackings**, kidnappings and bomb attacks. Terrorist groups are usually small, but they are often well funded and have access to the latest equipment. Fighting terrorism is difficult – potentially anyone visiting an airport, a government building or even a crowded café could be planning to hijack a plane, kill a government minister or set off a bomb.

Threats and challenges

This book looks at how weapons systems and the style of warfare are changing to meet the challenges of terrorism and guerrilla warfare. It also weighs up the benefits of hi-tech weapons – are the billions that rich governments spend on them worthwhile, or could the money be better used? The term **weapons of mass destruction (WMD)** is hardly ever out of the news these days. This book discusses the threats from WMD and what is being done to counteract them. It also looks at how technological advances that are in the pipeline might shape the fighting forces of the future.

Changing warfare

Like most wars throughout history, the two World Wars were **conventional wars**. However, in 1945 World War II in the Pacific ended in a very unconventional way, when the US air force dropped nuclear bombs on the Japanese cities of Hiroshima and Nagasaki. Japan knew that it had no defence against these **weapons of mass destruction**, and surrendered.

After World War II came the period known as the 'Cold War'. Although there was no actual fighting between their armies, Western Europe and North America were opposed to the Soviet Union and its allies. Huge numbers of troops were massed in East and West Germany, straddling the most sensitive border between the two groups of allies.

Since the end of the Cold War in the 1980s, there has been less need for large armed forces. Armies have been downsized, and there has been a shift to more flexible, rapid-response units for use in smaller armed conflicts, and to peacekeeping forces trained to work within a civilian population. Today's wars are more likely to be fought in the streets against **terrorists** and **guerrilla forces** rather than on remote battlefields. The skills and equipment required to fight an 'urban war' are very different to those used in conventional wars. Soldiers need to be trained to cope with the demands of this role.

Guerrilla warfare

Over the last 60 years there have been a number of conflicts involving guerrilla forces. For instance, in the Vietnam War (1964–1973) between North and South Vietnam, the USA sent armed forces to support the South Vietnamese government. Despite having a larger force and superior technology, the USA was unable to overcome the North Vietnamese, who used guerrilla tactics.

The Soviet Union had similar problems during the late 1970s when Soviet troops invaded Afghanistan and were challenged by guerrilla forces. Soviet military tactics were to carry out initial bombing raids followed by a massive **artillery** bombardment. Then the tanks would roll in.

After the terrorist attack on the Twin Towers in New York on 11 September 2001, US President George Bush declared a worldwide War on Terror.

During these initial attacks the guerrillas retreated into the mountains, only to reappear and ambush columns of troops and vehicles in narrow valleys. The Soviet forces changed tactics and started to use helicopter gunships with some success, but the guerrillas used missiles to bring down the helicopters. The war was unpopular with the Soviet people, so in 1989 the troops were withdrawn.

> 'We did not simply leave, we left with the war wrapped around the tracks of our tanks and the wheels of our vehicles, taking it home, and it flared up on our soil.'
>
> Russian Security Council Chief Alexander Lebed, on the Soviet withdrawal from Afghanistan in 1989

Terrorism

Terrorist groups have caused problems in many parts of the world over the last 60 years. From the 1960s onwards the Provisional IRA tried to overthrow British rule in Northern Ireland. In the early 1970s, the Black September group carried out many **hijackings** and kidnappings in support of an independent country for Palestinians. In the 1980s, al-Qaeda was set up to fight the Soviet Army when it occupied Afghanistan, and it has since become an international terrorist organization. On 11 September 2001, al-Qaeda launched a major attack on US soil when terrorists flew passenger airliners into the Twin Towers of the World Trade Center in New York, and the Pentagon in Washington. Thousands of people were killed.

New tactics

Terrorist tactics include hijacking, kidnapping and bombing targets such as airports and financial centres. Armed forces have had to develop new tactics to try and prevent terrorism. The British Army gained valuable experience in Northern Ireland while fighting the IRA. They learned how to patrol urban streets, assess difficult situations and detect and defuse bombs. This knowledge has been invaluable for peacekeeping duties in other countries.

Some conventional weapons have changed relatively little since World War II. Modern tanks (top) look much the same as those used in World War II (bottom), although they are more powerful, faster, better armed and better protected.

New technology

Some new weapons systems developed in the last 60 years have had a major impact on the nature of war. Probably the most important of these new types of weapon is the missile. Missiles are rockets, often with guidance systems, carrying an explosive warhead. They have changed the rules of warfare completely, because they allow attacks to be carried out from a great distance away. Once it took a battleship, firing from reasonably close range, to destroy another battleship. Now a missile fired from many kilometres away can achieve the same result.

Two other areas of technological change have opened up completely new ways of conducting warfare – **satellite** technology and computerization. Satellites allow commanders to talk almost instantaneously to troops anywhere around the world, to take aerial photographs without risking aircraft, and to eavesdrop on enemy communications. They can also provide accurate navigational information for missiles, bombs and soldiers (see pages 28–30). The development of small, powerful computers from the 1980s onwards has provided weapons with extremely accurate guidance systems. It has also made it possible to set up complex communications networks, which allow information from satellites, aircraft and other sources to be passed between military commanders and soldiers in the field.

Weapons of mass destruction

The latest missiles and bombs are precision weapons. As well as being more accurate and deadly in destroying their target, their use is intended to help minimize civilian damage and deaths. Weapons of mass destruction (WMD) are very different. These are weapons designed to kill large numbers of people indiscriminately. A WMD attack on a city, industrial centre or on agriculture would demoralize an enemy and could completely destroy its ability to fight a war.

Nuclear weapons

Nuclear weapons are the most destructive WMD. They can kill large numbers of people and destroy buildings, roads and other structures over a wide area. They also leave an area contaminated by **radioactive fallout**. However, nuclear weapons are difficult to manufacture. They need complex guidance systems, triggers and nuclear fuel such as **enriched uranium** or **plutonium**.

Biochemical weapons

Biological and chemical weapons do not have the immediate destructive power of a nuclear weapon. They are relatively crude weapons that leave buildings and other structures intact. Biological weapons are devices that carry disease-causing microorganisms (microbes), or **toxins** made by such microorganisms. Chemical weapons are dangerous chemicals that affect the skin, eyes, lungs, blood, nerves or other organs.

Real-time TV

During World War II there was no television or satellite technology to transmit pictures and reports almost instantly from the battlefront. People read about the war in newspapers or listened to reports on the radio, and the news they got could be several days old. Governments often censored war reports, minimizing any bad news and 'talking up' the successes.

By the time of the Falklands War in 1982, news reporting had radically changed. People saw TV footage of some of the action, including horrifying scenes such as the evacuation of severely injured soldiers after the bombing of the British landing craft, *Sir Galahad*. By the 1990s it was possible to provide live TV reporting direct from the front line, bringing the battlefield into people's living rooms.

During the 2003 Iraq War, many reporters travelled with a particular unit of soldiers throughout the war, giving them unprecedented access to the war zone.

The change in the reporting of wars has raised many issues. The speed of modern communications makes it difficult for governments to control what is seen by the public. It is not yet clear whether such images make us a more violent society or make people more aware of the dangers of warfare.

'For the first time ever in our history we not only have thousands – literally thousands – of journalists travelling with the troops but we have broadcast media behind what I would describe as enemy lines, reporting blow-by-blow what is happening.'

David Blunkett, UK Home Secretary, talking about media coverage of the 2003 Iraq War

Costly wars

The cost of modern warfare is immense. The 2003 Iraq War cost the USA at least US$20 billion, even though it lasted only a few weeks. The on-going cost of peacekeeping is estimated at US$4 billion, and the cost of returning troops and equipment will be a further US$5–7 billion. Advances in technology mean that although weapons are more powerful and more accurate, they are also more expensive. Tomahawk missiles can cost anything up to US$1 million each, and hundreds were fired within the first few days of the war.

Because the latest weapons are so complex and expensive, only the richest and most technically advanced countries can benefit from them. The richest country in the world, the USA, has by far the largest and most sophisticated armed forces. The armed forces of the UK, France, Germany, Australia and Japan are also technologically advanced, but much smaller than those of the USA. Countries such as Iraq have some powerful individual weapon systems and large numbers of troops, but they have little access to satellite technology and their communications networks are poor.

Some people question whether the costs of hi-tech weapons are justified. The money has to come from the government budget, which may mean that public services such as housing, education and health care have to be cut back to pay for weapons. Governments have to make difficult decisions as to whether it would be better to spend money on improving conditions for everybody at home rather than going to war.

'Every gun that is made, every warship launched, every rocket fired, signifies in the final sense a theft from those who hunger and are not fed, those who are cold and are not clothed.'

US President Dwight D Eisenhower, 1953

Biochemical weapons

Biological weapons (bioweapons) involve the release of disease-carrying microorganisms or the **toxins** that they produce. Chemical weapons use chemicals that harm the body. The use of bioweapons is not new. An early example of biological attack occurred in 1346, when bubonic plague infected Mongol troops retreating from Kaffa in the Crimea (now Southern Russia). The Mongols catapulted the corpses of plague victims into the city, where the disease claimed many victims. Survivors from Kaffa may have carried the disease back to Italy, and started the Black Death epidemic that killed almost a third of Europe's population.

Mustard gas, an early chemical weapon, was used in World War I. The Geneva Protocol of 1925 (see page 18) banned the use of chemical and biological weapons, but chemical agents were nonetheless used in the war between Iran and Iraq in the 1980s. **Terrorists** have also used chemical weapons. In 1995 a Japanese terrorist group released the **nerve agent** Sarin in the Tokyo subway (see page 18).

Bioweapons

The microorganisms used as biological weapons are bacteria or viruses that cause disease or serious poisoning from the toxins that they produce. A biological agent can either be released into the air, from where it gets into the body by being inhaled, or it can be used to contaminate food or drinking water. Some agents can be spread by contact, after touching contaminated surfaces.

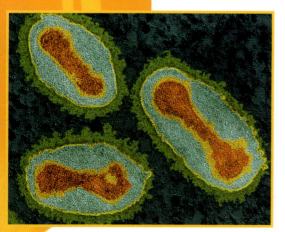

The smallpox virus, shown here, was eradicated in 1976. However a few laboratories around the world hold stocks of the virus and there are fears that terrorists could obtain these.

When bacteria or viruses enter the body, there is an **incubation period**, before symptoms appear. This may be days or weeks. During this time, the organisms continue to spread and infect more people before anyone is aware that a biological agent has been released. Toxins tend to cause illness or death within a few hours, or sometimes even minutes.

What makes a biological agent?

A biological agent needs to be highly infectious (easy to catch), and lethal. It should be able to survive in the environment for a long period of time, and it must be possible to produce it on a large scale. It is more effective if there is no treatment or **vaccine** for the disease.

The two most feared biological agents are anthrax and smallpox. Both are highly lethal – four out of every five people die from anthrax if it is untreated before the onset of serious symptoms, while one in three people infected with smallpox could die. Although there are vaccines for both diseases, only a limited number of them are available.

The following table shows the effects of six biological agents classified as being the highest risk to US national security (from the US Center for Disease Control).

Agent	Symptoms	Treatment
Anthrax	Early symptoms include fever, general weakness, coughing, difficulty breathing. Death can occur within 36 hours. Not contagious.	A vaccine is available but it is reserved for military use. If given early, antibiotics can prevent illness.
Botulinum toxin (toxin produced by bacteria *Clostridium botulinum*)	Blurred vision and difficulty in swallowing or speaking, followed by muscle paralysis. The victim suffocates and dies.	The toxin can be treated with an anti-toxin.
Pneumonic and bubonic plague	Symptoms occur within 1 to 6 days and include fever, coughing and difficulty breathing. Death is rare.	Treated with antibiotics.
Smallpox	Fever, headache and nausea for about 2 to 4 days. A spotty rash spreads over the body and blisters form. It is highly contagious.	A vaccination can prevent infection, but there is no effective treatment and 1 in 3 victims die.
Tularemia (rabbit fever)	One of the most infectious bacteria known. After 3 to 5 days, victims develop fever, headaches, chills. Inflammation and bleeding of the airways causes 1 in 3 to die.	Treated with antibiotics.
Viral haemorrhagic fevers e.g. Lassa fever and Ebola	Symptoms (fever, aches and diarrhoea) can appear from 3 days to 2 weeks. Haemorrhaging occurs from body tissues, mouth and nose.	Some strains respond to anti-viral drugs. If left untreated, between 30 and 90 per cent of victims die.

Chemical weapons

Chemical weapons are weapons that release toxic chemicals that attack the body through the lungs, skin or gut. Many chemical weapons are industrial chemicals that are safe in small amounts but lethal in large quantities. So chemical agents are abundant, easy to acquire, and relatively cheap.

Many modern chemical agents are designed to penetrate the skin. The thinner and the moister the skin, the greater the chances of penetration, so the eyes are particularly vulnerable to chemical agents. The lungs are also vulnerable and many chemical agents are designed to be inhaled.

Farmers use organophosphate pesticides to dip their sheep and protect them against parasites such as ticks. These sheep dips belong to the same group of chemicals as the nerve agents Sarin and VX gas.

There are five categories of chemical agent. They are nerve, blister, choking, blood and irritating agents.

Nerve agents

Nerve agents work by interfering with the transmission of nerve impulses. Nerves are vital to the body – they carry information from the senses to the brain, and transmit messages from the brain to the muscles. Exposure to a nerve gas leads to convulsions (violent and uncontrollable muscular contractions) followed by death when the muscles used to breathe are paralysed. Examples of nerve agents include Sarin, a chemical that acts by direct contact with the skin, and VX gas, which is inhaled. There are antidotes that counteract the effects of nerve agents, but they have to be injected immediately.

Blister agents

Blister agents cause burning and blistering of the skin and irritation of the eyes and lungs. If the lungs are badly affected they may fill with liquid and cause death. Symptoms can take between two and 24 hours to develop. Mustard gas is a blister agent that was widely used during World War I.

The dose of a blister agent needed to kill a person is about 50 times more than for a nerve agent, so blister agents are more likely to disable than to kill. The best treatment is to remove as much of the chemical as possible by washing, but there is no antidote.

Choking agents

Choking agents cause coughing, choking and headaches. Liquid can collect in the lungs and cause death. Examples of choking agents include the gases phosgene and chlorine. There are no treatments or antidotes for these agents.

Blood agents

Blood agents such as hydrogen cyanide starve the body of oxygen by stopping the transfer of oxygen from red blood cells to other cells in the body. A large dose causes vomiting, convulsions, breathing difficulties and death. There is no antidote as such, but injecting a sufferer with the chemical sodium thiosulphate turns the cyanide into a harmless substance that passes out in the urine.

Irritating agents

Irritating agents, such as tear gas, cause pain in the eyes, a flow of tears and difficulty in keeping the eyes open. They can irritate the mouth and nose which leads to vomiting, but they are not usually lethal.

> 'Biological or chemical agents are amenable to [can be used for] the waging of psychological warfare because of the horror and dread they can inspire. Even if the agents are not actually used, the fear of them can cause disruption, even panic.'
>
> World Health Organization report on Health Aspects of Biological and Chemical Weapons

Manufacturing chemical and biological weapons

The manufacture of chemical weapons employs virtually the same systems and processes as completely legal industrial products, such as pesticides. This means that industrial plants and equipment used to manufacture industrial chemicals can be switched easily to the manufacture of **weapons of mass destruction**.

Biological weapons are more difficult to produce than chemical weapons. Bacteria are usually cultured (grown) on a jelly-like substance in a covered glass dish. However, producing anthrax bacteria, for instance, is more complicated than simply growing a bacterial culture. The most effective bioweapon is an airborne spore (a resting form of the bacteria) that can be inhaled into the lungs. The spores have to be grown to the right size, and kept from clumping together when they are released.

Viruses need to grow on other living organisms – the 'flu virus, for instance, is grown in chicken eggs. Smallpox is difficult to grow and it is so deadly that it poses a very serious risk to laboratory workers that try to culture it.

A laboratory technician has to wear protective clothing and a face mask when handling pathogenic bacteria. The bacteria are cultured inside a sealed cabinet so that they cannot escape into the atmosphere.

Controlling the scientists

Biological and chemical weapons are developed by scientists. In the past, several countries funded research into such weapons, and more recently, countries such as Iraq have employed scientists to carry out research designed to produce biochemical weapons. Sometimes the weapons are a result of a spin-off from research into disease, or they may be discovered by scientists researching defences against biological or chemical attack.

In the past, it has been easy for people to obtain samples of bacteria and viruses. In some cases samples have gone missing from scientific laboratories, and nobody knows where they have ended up. However, since the terrorist attack on the Twin Towers in New York in 2001, governments in Europe and the USA have been tightening up the laws regarding research into disease-causing organisms. US scientists working on certain types of bacteria, viruses and toxins have to be given security clearance.

'Doctors and other scientists have an important role in prevention. They have a duty to persuade politicians and international agencies such as the UN to take this threat [of biological weapons] seriously and to take action to prevent the production of such weapons.'
British Medical Association in a statement about the
Biological Weapons Convention

Neuropharmacology

Research into the functioning of the brain has led to the development of drugs that affect our senses, emotions and moods, and even the way in which we control our body. This field of medicine is called neuropharmacology. Such drugs could be very useful chemical weapons. Imagine, for example, a chemical that could temporarily cause a person to lose the will to fight.

One such drug under development is 3-quinuclidinylbenzilate (BZ). This chemical causes the pupils to widen, makes short-distance vision worse and causes the heart to beat rapidly. At higher doses, it causes hallucinations and the victim may go into a coma. The effects can last for up to three weeks after the initial poisoning.

Biochemical warfare

Many countries have developed biological and chemical weapons in the past. Some armies have even used such weapons on the battlefield, for example during World War I and more recently in Iran and Iraq. However, since World War I there have been a number of treaties (agreements between countries) dealing with biochemical weapons. The first was the Geneva Protocol, signed in 1925, which prohibited the use of chemical or biological weapons in warfare. Another agreement, prohibiting the development, production and stockpiling of biological weapons, was signed in 1975. In 1993 the Chemical Weapons Convention agreed to eliminate the production and storage of chemical weapons.

Sarin attack

In the morning rush hour on 20 March 1995, an extreme religious group, known as the Aum Supreme Truth cult, carried out a chemical attack on the Tokyo subway. The nerve agent Sarin was released on three different trains. The terrorists concealed the Sarin in containers, which they punctured before leaving the trains. Sarin is a colourless and odourless gas, so it is difficult to detect. The gas killed 12 people and more than 3000 people were admitted to hospital. Fortunately, levels of exposure were low, and most patients were able to leave hospital quickly. Nine months before the Tokyo attack, the same group had spread Sarin in the city of Matsumoto, killing seven people.

Most countries have signed up to the agreements banning chemical and biological weapons, so they are unlikely to be used in a **conventional war**. Today, the greatest threat is that terrorist groups will use such weapons to cause widespread disease. In 1994, a natural outbreak of the plague in India resulted in hundreds of thousands of people fleeing the city of Surat. Many countries stopped flights to and from India, and restricted the import of Indian goods. An outbreak of plague caused by **terrorist** action would perhaps create even greater panic.

Just the possibility that terrorists might launch such an attack prompts countries to spend billions of pounds to protect themselves. For example, the UK government has spent more than £30 million on smallpox **vaccines**, in order to guard against the possibility of terrorists releasing the smallpox virus.

Delivering the agents

Biological and chemical weapons could be released on a battlefield. Under good conditions, a Scud missile warhead filled with the **nerve agent** Sarin could contaminate an area of 360 square kilometres – about the area of Inner London. If the missile were filled with botulinum **toxin** instead, it could contaminate an area more than 16 times larger – more than the whole area of Greater London. However, the use of these weapons on the battlefield is risky. A change in the wind can easily carry the agent back over one's own troops and there is the possibility of contaminating a civilian population.

Scud missiles are medium-range missiles originally made in the Soviet Union in the 1960s. During the 1980s Iraq developed longer-range (up to 700 km) versions of the Scud, but they had small warheads and often broke up in flight.

SARS

In 2002, an outbreak of a flu-like illness called SARS (Severe Acute Respiratory Syndrome) showed how easily a biological agent could spread. Although this SARS outbreak was natural, the deliberate release of a biological agent could spread in a similar way.

The SARS virus was first diagnosed in China in 2003. Over the next few months, the illness spread to more than 20 countries, infecting over 8000 people. Luckily many of those infected recovered, but even so over 800 people died. The disease was eventually contained by isolating both people infected with SARS and those suspected of having the disease. This prevented more people from becoming infected.

SARS spread quickly because in today's world people travel widely. The outbreak caused much panic and badly affected business. Many people in Hong Kong, for example, left the territory and may have carried the virus to unaffected parts of the world. People cancelled holidays and business trips to infected cities, and far fewer people took flights to Asia.

At the height of the SARS outbreak of 2003, many people in cities at risk, such as Hong Kong, began wearing protective face masks to protect them from inhalation of the SARS virus.

Without warning

Terrorists release biochemical weapons without warning, so the population is not protected. Toxins can be sprayed into closed spaces such as subways or placed in the air-conditioning systems of large buildings. Toxins can also be introduced into foodstuffs or water supplies.

The most-feared method is an airborne attack which can spread biological or chemical toxins over a large area. A bomb or missile explosion over a city centre, a crop-spraying plane, a vehicle spraying a fine mist, or small bombs released in crowded areas could all cause huge loss of life.

Effectiveness

Biological weapons are potentially much more lethal than chemical weapons. Just a few kilograms of biological agent have the potential to devastate a population. For example, the release of 90 kilograms of anthrax spores upwind of a major city could kill up to 3 million people. By contrast, it would take several tonnes of chemical agent to kill a few thousand people.

Most biological agents are non-persistent and break down rapidly, while chemical agents can remain active for much longer. Anthrax is an exception to this rule, because its spores can remain active in soil for decades. When anthrax was tested in 1942 on Gruinard Island, Scotland, the persistence of the spores made it unsafe for anyone to live there for 48 years.

Protective clothing

Soldiers at risk from a biochemical attack can put on protective, anti nuclear, biological and chemical (NBC) suits if they have warning. NBC suits are made from layers of treated woven fabric, used to disperse liquid, and a charcoal-based layer to provide absorption. They are completely impermeable to gas or fluid, and are highly resistant to tearing. Such suits give protection against a chemical attack for at least six hours. A gas mask filters the air to protect against chemical agents, radioactive particles, bacteria and viruses.

Soldiers in full NBC suits. Although such suits provide good protection from chemical and biological weapons, they are hot and awkward to wear.

When wearing full NBC protection, the performance of a soldier is seriously affected, as it is hard to see, hear and breathe, and it is very tiring to move about.

Theatre attack

In October 2002, about 50 armed fighters stormed the Dubrovka theatre in Moscow and took more than 700 people hostage. The fighters demanded that Russia withdraw all Russian troops from Chechnya, a province in southern Russia that was fighting to become an independent country. In exchange, the fighters would release all the hostages safely.

Russian soldiers surrounded the theatre, and after three days the government sent in special forces to free the hostages. The fighters had explosives strapped to their bodies, so the special forces used a gas called Fentanyl, a fast-acting drug that causes people to lose consciousness, to put them out of action. Tragically, the gas proved to be fatal for some of the people who were near the places where the gas was pumped, in who received very high doses of the gas. More than 120 hostages were killed during the siege, all but two of them by Fentanyl. Dozens more people required hospital treatment for the effects of the gas.

Until this incident, Fentanyl was thought to be a fairly safe chemical agent. Unfortunately it is impossible to distinguish exactly between **non-lethal** and lethal agents, since the lethality depends upon such things as how much gas a person is exposed to, and their age and general state of health.

Detecting biochemical weapons

Releasing biochemical weapons does not require sophisticated equipment, but detecting them is another matter. Currently, British troops carry two types of chemical detector paper to detect liquid chemicals. The 'one-colour detector paper' changes colour when it comes into contact with any harmful liquid chemical. The 'three-colour detector paper' can identify two types of nerve agent and one blister agent, each of which turn the paper a different colour. Gases are detected using a more complicated device, which sucks air through tubes containing indicator chemicals.

Research is under way to develop a much more sophisticated system of **sensors** that will detect the presence of biological and chemical agents in the air. The sensors trap targeted chemicals, analyse them and send a signal to a control centre. The sensors could be mounted on military vehicles, creating a mobile battlefield sensor network.

Similar sensors could be used in homes, offices and airports, just as smoke alarms are used today. They could be placed on towers, pylons and large buildings and linked to a control centre. Once an agent was detected, computers would use weather data to predict the spread of the agent and to warn populations.

A system of sensors already exists that can track the spread of insecticides and fertilizers. Trial chemical sensor networks are being placed in the Boston and Washington subways, at the San Francisco airport and on the Miami docks in the USA.

> 'The goal for all the government efforts, perhaps three to five years out, is to deploy a highly accurate yet low-cost network of sensors that in a couple of minutes could tell you if an agent is present, in what concentration and something about the agent. But the technology for that doesn't really exist yet.'
>
> Duane Lindner, director of the Sandia
> National Laboratory, California, USA

Nuclear weapons

History was made during World War II on 16 July 1945, when the first nuclear bomb, code-named Trinity, was exploded in New Mexico, USA. A few weeks later war in the Pacific came to a sudden end when the US detonated two nuclear bombs, over Hiroshima and Nagasaki in Japan. These two powerful bombs destroyed the cities and killed about 200,000 people.

Nuclear bombs are extremely powerful weapons. They make use of the tremendous energy that is locked up in **atoms**. There are two ways that nuclear energy can be released from an atom – by **nuclear fusion**, or by **nuclear fission** (see panel).

Nuclear damage

A nuclear bomb causes immense damage. This is caused by a wave of intense heat from the explosion, the pressure from the shock wave created by the blast, and by **radiation**. Fine **radioactive** particles of dust and debris are then created, which fall back to the ground. The degree of damage depends upon the distance from the centre of the bomb blast, which is called ground zero. The closer to ground zero, the more severe the destruction.

At ground zero, everything is immediately vaporized by the high temperatures. Away from ground zero, most casualties are due to burns from the heat and ultraviolet radiation, injuries from collapsing buildings and exposure to high levels of radiation. In the short term, exposure to radiation causes severe skin burns, sickness, fatigue and inflammation of the mouth and gut. In the long term, people exposed to radiation are more likely to suffer from cancers, and women may give birth to deformed babies.

'Atomic bombs are primarily a means for the ruthless annihilation of cities. Once they were introduced as an instrument of war it would be difficult to resist for long the temptation of putting them to such use.'

Leo Szilard and 58 co-signers of a petition to the President of the United States, 3 July 1945 concerning the proposed use of atomic weapons against Japan.

Fission and fusion

There are two types of nuclear reaction – fission and fusion. An atom consists of a small, heavy nucleus at the centre, surrounded by a cloud of much lighter, tiny electrons. The nucleus contains two kinds of particles called protons and **neutrons**. In a fission reaction the nucleus of an atom is split into two smaller fragments. In a fusion reaction two smaller atoms fuse (their nuclei join) to form a larger atom.

Fission bombs work by splitting the nuclei of **plutonium**. These atoms are large and unstable, and if they are split energy is released. Fission is achieved by bombarding plutonium with fast-moving neutrons. Each nucleus that splits releases energy and more neutrons. These neutrons collide with other plutonium atoms, causing them to split too. This sets off a chain reaction, with more and more nuclei being split. When this occurs, a vast amount of energy is released and a massive explosion results.

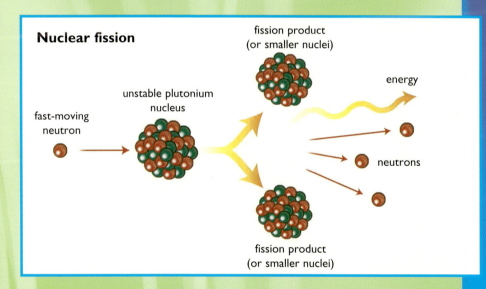

Nuclear fission

fast-moving neutron

unstable plutonium nucleus

fission product (or smaller nuclei)

energy

neutrons

fission product (or smaller nuclei)

Fission bombs are not as powerful as the hydrogen or thermonuclear bomb, which is a fusion bomb. In the fusion reaction, two hydrogen atoms collide at very high speeds and join to make helium. The fusion reaction only starts at extremely high temperatures, so a small fission bomb has to be exploded to set off the fusion bomb. A hydrogen bomb explosion creates an extremely hot zone near its centre, which vaporizes just about any material and causes a destructive shock wave to travel outwards.

The dirty bomb

There is great concern around the world that **terrorist** groups could acquire a small amount of nuclear fuel and turn it into a workable nuclear bomb.

Nuclear weapons are sophisticated devices that require large-scale manufacturing facilities, but it is relatively easy to make a 'dirty bomb', or radiological dispersion bomb. This is a bomb that consists of an explosive surrounded by radioactive material. A dirty bomb is a lot cruder and cheaper than a nuclear bomb, and it is less effective, but the detonation of such a bomb would cause immense fear and panic. It would not kill many people straight away, but the bomb would spread radioactive material in a dust cloud that could be carried long distances by the wind. The increased radiation exposure could kill many people in the long term, as it increases the risk of cancer. Just the fear of radioactive contamination could terrorize a large population.

Nuclear testing

Testing is part of a nuclear weapons programme. Nuclear bombs have been exploded under test conditions in the air, underwater and underground. Since 16 July 1945 there have been more than 2000 nuclear tests worldwide – the equivalent of one test occurring somewhere in the world every nine days. It is estimated that the total yield (the amount of energy released) from all the atmospheric nuclear weapons tests carried out is 510 megatons – the equivalent of nearly 35,000 bombs the size of the one dropped on Hiroshima.

Mini-nukes

Recent newspaper reports have indicated that the American military is investigating the use of small nuclear weapons nicknamed 'mini-nukes'. Such weapons could be used to attack bunkers of nuclear, chemical or biological materials buried deep underground. Even though this is just an idea, many people are already voicing their objections to new nuclear weapons of any kind being developed. The US government, on the other hand, argues that it is faced with the horror of enemies using **WMD** and has to consider some extreme ideas to protect its population.

'The US is pressing the world to get rid of nuclear weapons yet is doing the exact opposite itself.'

Ben Miller, a spokesman for the Campaign for
Nuclear Disarmament

Wherever nuclear weapons testing has occurred there have been environmental problems. Almost 4000 kilograms of plutonium has been left in the ground as a result of all the underground nuclear tests that have been carried out. Another 4000 kilograms of plutonium has been released into the atmosphere. Radioactivity has leaked into ground water from underground nuclear tests, and large areas of land have been left uninhabitable.

In 1996 the Comprehensive Test Ban Treaty was drawn up. It prohibits any nuclear explosion, whether for weapons or peaceful purposes. However, the treaty does not become effective until it is agreed by all eight nuclear nations and this has not yet happened.

Many nuclear tests have been carried out on remote islands in the Pacific Ocean. There were over 180 test explosions at just two sites, Moruroa and Fangataufa atolls. Despite their remote location, these test explosions have caused a range of environmental and human health problems.

Smart technology

Smart weapons are bombs, missiles and other weapons that can home in on specific targets with great accuracy, and even respond to changes on the battlefield. These weapons are revolutionizing warfare. For instance, during World War II, 650 bombs were needed to destroy a stationary target. By the 1992 Gulf War, just four smart bombs were needed to destroy an equivalent target. Nowadays, as much as 80 per cent of munitions used by US and UK forces are smart. Whilst the use of smart weapons means that there are fewer civilian and military casualties, they cost a great deal more than conventional weapons. For example, British fighter-bombers are equipped with **laser**-guided smart bombs, such as the Paveway, each of which costs about £40,000.

Spotting a target

Smart weapons have **sensors** that pick up information about their surroundings, and an information processor (a built-in computer) to interpret the information. For instance, smart artillery shells that are designed to recognize and attack tanks would be equipped with magnetic sensors that can detect iron and steel. The information processor might be programmed to recognize a particular size of signal as being 'tank-like'. It can then slightly alter the path of the shell so that it is directed towards the target signal. Shells or missiles that are guided in this way are referred to as precision guided munitions (PGM).

Smart bombs

Smart bombs have a guidance system to direct the bomb to its target. There are four types of guidance: electro-optical, infrared, **global positioning system (GPS)** (see panel on page 29) and laser guidance.

Laser guidance is one of the most accurate systems. A laser-guided bomb is released in the vicinity of the target at the correct height and angle. A laser beam is pointed at the target, either by the plane that dropped the bomb, by a second aircraft or by a soldier on the ground. This creates a small spot of light on the target. The laser bomb has a moveable, 'electronic eye' that can detect this spot of light. The bomb's information processor adjusts the weapon's descent towards its target by moving tiny wings on the bomb's nose.

The main limitation of laser-guided bombs is the need for a clear line of sight from laser to target and target to bomb. In practice this means that such weapons cannot be used if it is cloudy, raining or if there is heavy smoke. Bombs that make use of the GPS do not suffer from these problems, but they do not have quite the accuracy of laser-guided weapons.

Global positioning system

The global positioning system (GPS) is a network of navigational **satellites** that enables a GPS user to find their position with great accuracy. The system uses a network of 24 satellites, orbiting at an altitude of about 20,000 kilometres. The satellite network is organized so that every point on Earth is within range of at least four satellites. The satellites send out a stream of digital signals that can be picked up by a GPS receiver. The receiver compares the time it takes for a signal to reach it from each of the four satellites. From this information, the receiver can calculate its position.

GPS satellites are operated by the US military. They transmit two types of signal. One type is for civilian use, while the other signal is encrypted (coded), and is solely for military purposes. The difference between the two is in their accuracy. The civilian signal is normally accurate to about 16 metres, but in times of war the signal can be downgraded so that it is only accurate to about 100 metres. This is to prevent enemy forces from being able to benefit from the civilian GPS system.

The military GPS signal can be made more accurate than the civilian system. During the 2003 Iraq War, engineers tweaked the system to give military GPS receivers, such as those in precision guided weapons, an accuracy of about three metres.

Satellite-guided bombs

A bomb called the joint direct attack munition (JDAM) is guided by GPS. Target coordinates are normally loaded before the aircraft takes off, although the flight crew can alter them manually before the bomb is released. Once released, the bomb's GPS guides it to the target regardless of weather conditions. GPS signals can be jammed, or made unintelligible by the enemy. If this happens, the JDAM has a backup **inertial navigation system** that it can use to reach its target. Although JDAM bombs are much cheaper than laser-guided weapons, (and it is possible to convert 'dumb' bombs into JDAMs), they are not as accurate. However, they perform better in poor weather conditions.

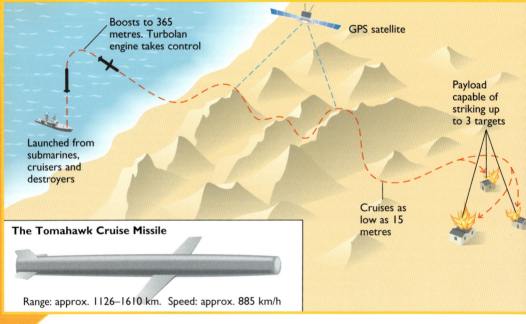

Boosts to 365 metres. Turbolan engine takes control

GPS satellite

Launched from submarines, cruisers and destroyers

Payload capable of striking up to 3 targets

Cruises as low as 15 metres

The Tomahawk Cruise Missile

Range: approx. 1126–1610 km. Speed: approx. 885 km/h

The US Tomahawk missile is a smart **cruise missile** that uses GPS navigation combined with a camera system for identifying targets. This makes it an extremely accurate weapon.

Missing the target

Even laser-guided missiles can miss their target. In the 2003 Iraq War, more than 8000 'precision-guided' missiles were used. About ten per cent of these weapons did not hit their intended target. There were many reasons for these failures, including technical and mechanical failures, and human error.

Problems most often arise when targets are in urban areas, where accuracy is essential to avoid civilian casualties. Sometimes military bases are deliberately set up in towns and cities, to make them more difficult to target. Sometimes the enemy may put out false information about the location of their bases and so the wrong targets may be hit.

'No weapons system is foolproof. We'll always have one or two that go off target.'

Lieutenant Commander Charles Owens, spokesman for US Central Command, discussing the use of precision-guided missiles in the 2003 Iraq War

The Apache attack helicopter is one of the most advanced helicopters in the world. It is equipped with a range of smart weapon systems, including fire-control **radar**. This can search for targets, decide on their importance, and use the information to control the firing of the helicopter's missiles. Not only can it do these things in almost all weathers, but the radar also has a low power output, making it very hard for the enemy to detect.

Automatic target recognition

Although smart weapons have tremendous capabilities, their ability to accurately recognize targets without human help is still limited. A human recognizes an object through a combination of shape, pattern and other characteristics, which the brain compares with similar objects seen in the past. Researchers are now trying to teach computers to recognize targets in the same way. However, the human brain is still much better at matching patterns and, most importantly, has much better judgment in uncertain conditions. Smart weapons have to be told what to do if they are unsure about the identity of a target. Is it a tank? A friend or foe? Is it a vehicle carrying civilians or enemy soldiers? Programming a weapon to attack only if it is absolutely sure of its target may mean that the weapon is ineffective. On the other hand, programming weapons to attack even when they are unsure of the target could lead to many civilian casualties and troops killed by 'friendly fire'.

Adaptive materials

Adaptive materials are helping to improve weapon design and performance. Adaptive materials have unusual characteristics. They can change shape if exposed to heat, an electric current or an electromagnetic charge. The change in shape can be used to morph, or twist, a structure into a new shape. Wings made with adaptive materials, for example, might change shape at take-off and landing, just as a bird can change the shape of its wings. This would make it possible for aircraft to take off and land on much shorter runways.

Adaptive materials are not yet strong enough to be used for large, heavy airplane wings. They are more likely to be used initially in small unmanned vehicles, missiles and smart weapons.

Piezoelectric materials

Piezoelectric materials are one kind of adaptive material. A piezoelectric material is one that changes shape when an electric current is passed through it. At present, the most common piezoelectric materials are quartz crystals, which vibrate when a changing electric signal is passed through them. Such crystals are used in quartz watches, microphones, small loudspeakers and many other devices.

Other piezoelectric materials are now being developed for use in helicopter rotors. The piezoelectric materials replace mechanical parts in order to reduce vibration. In one study in 1997, adaptive materials were used to reduce the number of components in a helicopter rotor from 94 to 5. The total weight of the rotor was reduced by 8 per cent, and a flight test showed that air speed was improved by 18 per cent.

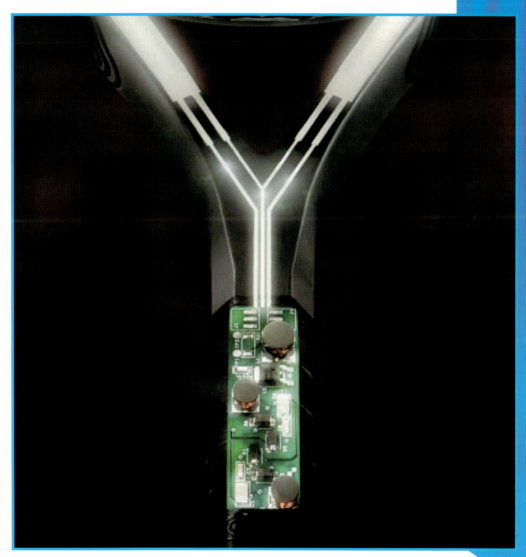

Piezoelectric materials in the neck of a hi-tech tennis racket are stimulated when a ball hits the strings. This sends a message to the microchip in the handle, which sends a signal back and makes the neck of the racket stiffer – all in less than a millisecond. Changing the properties of the racket neck in this way gives more power to the return stroke, and cuts down uncomfortable vibrations in the handle.

Hi-tech weapons

Smart weapons are only part of a whole new generation of weapons developed in countries such as the USA, the UK and Australia. These hi-tech weapons mean that fewer troops need to be put on to the battlefield. There have also been great advances in **stealth** technology – the art of making aircraft, ships and road vehicles harder for the enemy to detect.

Thermobaric weapons

While smart weapons are designed for pinpoint accuracy, the 'Fuel Air Explosive' (FAE), or **thermobaric** weapon, is all about power. When it explodes, the FAE creates a huge fireball and a massive blast wave that travels at 3000 metres per second. Such a blast can travel round corners and upwards through openings between building floors.

Thermobaric weapons were used by the USA against Afghan fighters in the 2002 war in Afghanistan. The fighters were hiding in caves, beyond the reach of traditional bombs.

Close to the blast centre, temperatures can reach 2500°C or more and pressures can be up to 30 times normal atmospheric pressure. Such pressures literally crush people to death. Thermobaric bombs are effective against soldiers, equipment, underground storage areas, communication centres, urban strong points and even minefields. They can also be used to destroy crops or vegetation.

Mother of All Bombs

There is no doubt that thermobaric weapons are highly effective but they produce horrifying scenes as the battlefield is turned into a huge fireball. They have been nicknamed the MOAB – the Mother Of All Bombs. The power of a thermobaric weapon is comparable to that of a nuclear bomb, and some people think that they should be classed as **weapons of mass destruction**. Unfortunately there are no international laws prohibiting the use of these bombs.

Blackout bombs

Modern armies rely on electricity for communications, power and control systems. So, not surprisingly, weapons have been developed to attack electrical systems. One such weapon is the blackout bomb. These bombs release a mass of fine carbon-fibre or fibreglass filaments coated with a conductive metal film. If they are exploded near a communications vehicle for example, the filaments touch the communication masts and short them out, causing temporary loss of communications. However, if the filaments are brushed off, communications can usually be restored. Blackout bombs can also be used to knock out power grids and disrupt civilian power supplies.

Stealth technology

The term 'stealth' is usually applied to vehicles that have been specifically designed to be hard for an enemy to detect. Today there are stealth aircraft and stealth ships, and other applications are under development. Objects that are stealthy often have an extraordinary shape, for example the angular US F117A Nighthawk stealth fighter and the smoothly rounded contours of the B2 Spirit bomber.

Difficult to detect

A common misunderstanding is that stealth vehicles are invisible to **radar** or infrared (heat) detectors. In fact it is not possible to completely hide a large vehicle, but by using special materials and careful design, detection can be made very difficult. The engines of a stealth vehicle are designed to run cool, so that they are very hard to detect using infrared **sensors**. The engine intakes are shrouded (partly covered), which greatly reduces the vehicle's radar signal. Parts of the aircraft are made from radar-absorbing materials, and panels are angled to send radar beams off at odd angles rather than bouncing them straight back to the radar receiver.

The key weakness of stealth aircraft and other stealth vehicles is that by day they can be seen as easily as any other vehicle. In the James Bond film *Die Another Day*, Bond's Aston Martin car is equipped with a system that projects an image of the surroundings on to the car, making it invisible. Such a system of 'active camouflage' is actually under development in the laboratory. The idea is to create an image of the background on the skin of an aircraft, or ship, making it 'disappear'. This might be done by projecting a photograph or video on to a

The unusual angular shape of the stealth fighter means that radar beams are bounced off it at odd angles. This means it is not picked up by the radar receiver.

surface, or by using a sort of 'chameleon skin' system that could change colour. Although the idea is quite simple, putting it into practice is far more difficult, and it will be many years before any practical active camouflage system is developed.

Depleted uranium

Most tanks use two kinds of ammunition; high explosive, and armour-piercing (AP). High explosive rounds rely on explosive force to destroy another tank or building, but AP rounds are designed solely for destroying armoured vehicles. They fire a very dense, sharply pointed rod at very high velocity, which can penetrate armour. The denser the material from which the rod is made, the more easily it penetrates armour. **Depleted uranium (DU)** is one of the densest materials known. Armour-piercing ammunition made with DU is very effective, so fewer rounds are needed to destroy an enemy armoured vehicle. Fewer rounds means less money is spent. However there is a big environmental and health cost. DU is a by-product of the nuclear industry and its dust is toxic. Exposure to just 0.01g in one week can cause health problems.

During the Gulf War in 1991, thousands of DU rounds were fired, each round creating as much as 3.1kg of **radioactive** dust. This **toxic** dust is insoluble and can remain in the ground or in the body for years. It is believed that over 400,000 US troops may have entered areas that contained DU dust. The civilian population were probably also affected when they moved back into towns and villages contaminated by the dust. The effects of DU on the health are not immediate. It can cause cancers, but these may take 10 or 20 years to develop. Despite concerns about the health effects of DU, these weapons were used in the 2003 war in Iraq.

Rounds of armour-piercing amunition containing DU, on the battlefield.

Hi-tech tanks

When we think of **ceramics** we usually think of pottery, but ceramics are not always so delicate. Specially formulated ceramics can be lightweight and extremely tough. The latest British tank and US tanks use a **composite** armour made from two layers of steel sandwiching a layer of ceramic. When an explosive shell strikes the armour, the ceramic material shatters, producing an outward expansion that counteracts the inward force of the explosive shell.

The Russians have developed a different approach to tank protection, using a system known as explosive reactive armour. This armour is made up from bricks of explosive encased by metal plates, which sit on top of the conventional steel armour. If a shell hits the reactive armour, the explosive detonates and forces the metal plates outwards, protecting the armour beneath.

Land mines

Land mines are probably the most hated and feared weapons of recent wars, because of their indiscriminate killing of innocent civilians. Land mines and anti-personnel mines can remain active many years after a war has ended and are hard to detect, especially if they are made of plastic. Minefields are often unmarked, so they are difficult to identify. Every year since 2000 there have been 15,000 to 20,000 new land mine casualties. The charity organization, UNICEF estimates that up to 40 per cent of all land mine victims are children under the age of 15. The Ottawa Convention, a treaty banning mines, came into being in 1999, and has been signed by over 143 countries. Since then more than 34 million stockpiled anti-personnel mines have been destroyed.

Alternative systems are now being developed to keep people out of certain areas. The Ottawa Convention states that any replacement systems must be set off by a human command rather than triggered automatically. One idea being developed in Australia is a system of pods placed in strategic positions throughout the area to be protected. Each pod contains either sensors or ammunition and is linked to a command centre by radio. When a sensor detects a potential target, a signal is sent to the command centre for verification. This means that the weapons are only fired at the right moment.

These land mine victims in Afghanistan have been fitted with new artificial legs. An estimated 24,000 people are killed or injured by land mines each year.

Non-lethal weapons

Several different kinds of **non-lethal weapon** are currently being developed. One class of non-lethal weapons are 'pain beams' that create extreme pain. These weapons work by using electromagnetic energy to heat up the surface of the skin. A transmitter emits a narrow beam of radio waves, rather like those from a microwave oven. The beam penetrates just under the surface of the skin and causes a painful sensation, like touching a hot light bulb. The pain beam does not cause permanent burning of the skin, although repeated exposure does leave the skin feeling tender.

Other examples of non-lethal weapons include **laser** dazzle weapons and infrasound. Laser dazzle weapons are laser beams designed to temporarily or permanently blind enemy soldiers from a distance. Research has also been carried out into using very low sounds (infrasound) as a weapon. Infrasound can cause people to be violently sick and convulsed with muscular spasms.

Communication and intelligence gathering

Ever since the earliest days of organized fighting, commanders have recognized the need for good communications with their troops and accurate **intelligence** about the enemy's intentions. Good communications are essential, because they are the way that commanders find out what is happening on the battlefield, and send out commands to units in the field. Intelligence is vital, because the more that military commanders can find out about what the enemy is doing, the better they can plan their defence or attack.

At the heart of both good communications and good intelligence is the rapid transmission of information, whether it is a request for more ammunition, an order to **artillery** to change their target, or a report of an enemy attack.

Unmanned spy planes

Since the invention of aircraft, one of the most important sources of intelligence for military commanders has been aerial images. During the two World Wars, this information came from manned aircraft flying dangerous missions over enemy territory. The advent of **satellites** during the 1960s made it possible to get fairly detailed images of any part of the Earth, but spy planes were still important for fine detail.

Today, unmanned aerial vehicles (UAVs) have in many cases replaced spy planes for information-gathering. They are used to fly over enemy territory and send back information. They are either remote-controlled or autonomous (self-controlled). The latest UAVs carry highly sophisticated software for controlling their **sensors** and weapons to defend themselves against attack.

UAVs are far more than simply radio-controlled aircraft. A recent model, the Predator UAV, weighs 4.5 tonnes and carries a range of equipment for collecting information. This includes **radar**, TV cameras, infrared and **laser** systems that give it excellent 'night vision'. It also carries a datalink – a satellite communications linking system for rapidly sending the information it gathers back to base. The Predator can fly for up to 32 hours before refuelling. It can detect and track targets, and relay data back to a command post almost as it is gathered. Another form of the Predator, the hunter-killer variant, can not only send back information about enemy targets, it can also attack targets and defend itself against attack with a range of missiles.

The unmanned Predator flies at altitudes of up to 8000 metres to avoid shoulder-fired weapons.

Autonomous underwater vehicles

Most people are familiar with robot submersibles – undersea vehicles that are remotely controlled by an operator at the surface. Researchers are now working on developing autonomous underwater vehicles (AUVs) that have sufficient built-in intelligence to be able to operate fully automatically over great distances – only establishing communications with base when they need to transmit or receive information. Some AUVs will be able to navigate accurately, find their way along enemy coastlines and into harbours, detect enemy ship movements and report back by satellite. Others will be fighting vehicles rather than intelligence-gatherers, able to detect, track and attack an enemy submarine.

'There may come a time, thanks to AUVs, when very few people are involved in violent action.'
The Office of Naval Research in Arlington, Virginia, USA

Electronic warfare

Electronic warfare (EW) is an important part of intelligence. Passive EW involves intercepting enemy communications signals and analysing them to find out what the enemy is doing. Active EW involves transmitting signals that **jam** enemy communications or deceive the enemy. Jamming systems can either be used offensively, to disrupt enemy communications when an attack starts, or defensively, for instance to prevent the radar tracking system of an enemy missile system from locking-on to an aircraft.

Most military communications are encrypted (coded), and the codes are often hard, if not impossible, to break. But information can be gained from such messages even if they cannot be understood.

The EA-6B Prowler carries out electronic counter-measures such as jamming, enemy detection and identification. It is armed with high-speed anti-radiation missiles (HARM) that can neutralize enemy radar sites.

Modern EW systems can use direction-finding equipment to calculate the location of transmitting stations. They can also analyze the type and pattern of the signals. For example, a lot of transmissions from one area may indicate the presence of a headquarters.

Deception is equally important in electronic warfare. For example, it is possible to send out dummy radio and radar transmissions to fool the enemy into thinking that they are picking up signals from a command centre. Meanwhile, the real headquarters, in another place entirely, operates under strict radio silence.

Network-centric warfare

In modern warfare, computers are a central part of communications and information-gathering systems. Portable computer systems currently used by soldiers allow them to receive orders and information from command centres, and to send information back. Communications are continually improving – mobile phones can now be used to transmit photos and recorded sound files as well as speech and text messages.

Military planners envisage that soon all the elements of a military force – command centres, soldiers and vehicles on the ground, aircraft and UAVs – will be linked together by a mobile 'Internet'. This is called network-centric warfare (NCW). It will give commanders the ability to launch air strikes or plan and control troop movements from anywhere on the battlefield. At all times they will have a complete picture of what is going on.

Networking information

Each element (computer, sensor or weapon) in the NCW network would 'publish' its own capabilities and the information it holds, so that the other computers on the network can use it. Each element would also be able to extract information it needs from other parts of the network. For example, troops on the ground might want to access the latest photographs and other images of their target area from satellites and aircraft. Once they reach the target area they will be able to add their own information about the position of friendly and hostile forces. Commanders and troops would have a better awareness of events on the battlefield, which should reduce the danger of casualties from friendly fire.

Fast Tactical Imagery

Aircraft such as the US F-14 Tomcat fighter are already equipped with video recorders that can record up to two hours of video from weapons and sensors. Pilots can also play back images, maps and other information about their mission. In addition, a system known as Fast Tactical Imagery (FTI) allows images and target coordinates to be transmitted directly to or received from other aircraft and command centres while in flight. In the future, the aircraft will be able to upload even more information from anywhere on the battlefield.

Problems still to solve

Many questions still need to be addressed to create a successful NCW system. For example, how should priorities be allocated to information? Should some capacity on the network be reserved for 'important' messages? What happens if there is a sudden burst of communications,

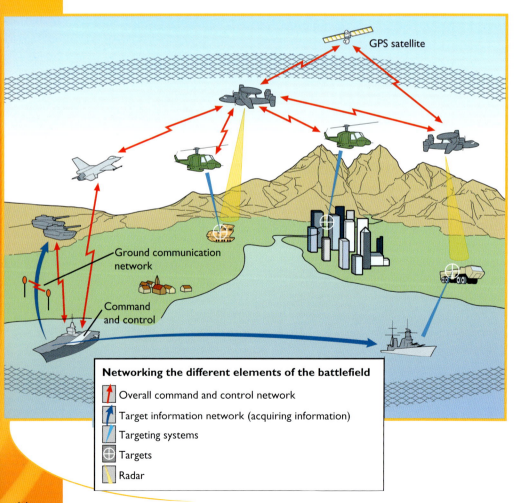

GPS satellite

Ground communication network

Command and control

Networking the different elements of the battlefield

- Overall command and control network
- Target information network (acquiring information)
- Targeting systems
- ⊕ Targets
- Radar

such as might occur when an attack takes place, with many units sending high-priority messages? Other issues include how to keep the network working properly when links are lost, and how to protect classified data from unauthorized use by both friends and enemies.

Disrupting the system

We have all seen how computer viruses can disrupt the flow of information on the Internet, and an NCW network could be just as vulnerable. Already there are ways and means to disrupt the systems that NCW will rely upon. For instance, a Russian company has developed a device that can block **GPS** signals from a distance of several kilometres. NCW is a new technology, and there are currently more questions than answers.

Perhaps the biggest vulnerability of the NCW system is the reliance on commercial satellites that are not under direct military control. In July 2002, a religious protest group managed to get control of China's key telecommunications satellites and prevented the satellite from sending out television and radio signals. If such a satellite was part of an NCW system, such an event could cause huge problems.

However, the main problem with NCW is that it is designed to work in a **conventional** battlefield situation. The idea needs to be adapted to be able to deal with peacekeeping operations, such as those carried out by the allied **coalition** troops in Afghanistan and Iraq, and for operations against **terrorism** and **guerrilla forces**.

Internet and terrorism

Technological advances are not just restricted to military systems. Civilian systems also benefit from the advance in military technology, and this means that terrorists can take advantage of them. The Internet has given terrorists access to improved communications, systems for coding their messages, imaging systems and global connections. Counter-terrorist organizations in Australia, Europe and North America are aware that terrorist groups make use of the Internet in this way, and they constantly monitor the Internet to try and pick up information of possible terrorist plots.

Another possibility is that terrorists and other rogue groups could achieve some of their aims by disrupting the Internet. With so many businesses depending on the Internet, the release of a computer virus or worm causes much economic damage.

Future soldier

Hi-tech weapons may be very effective on the battlefield, but wars cannot be won with just weapons. Soldiers are still needed, and technological development is going to transform the soldier of the future.

The training of soldiers is just as important as technology. There is no point investing in **smart** weapon systems and mobile networks if soldiers cannot use them. Currently, it is mostly special forces such as the British SAS and the US Green Berets that receive specialist training for **guerrilla** warfare, counter-terrorism, or **surveillance** operations to gather **intelligence**. However, increasingly, ordinary soldiers are trained to carry out peace-keeping and counter-insurgency operations in urban environments.

An example of a helmet with head-up displays that include thermal imaging capability, GPS targeting and sighting, and communications links.

Improved clothing

The separate sets of clothing (combat kit, NBC suit and additional warm clothing) that a soldier needs are a significant weight to carry. The next generation of military clothing could change all this. Uniforms will be much lighter and made up of multiple layers. The outer layers will provide NBC and environmental protection, the middle layers will have heating and cooling ducts to keep the soldier warm but not too hot, and a inner 'physiological layer' will monitor heartbeat, temperature, and so on. The suit will be powered by a fuel cell.

Helmets are likely to change, too. Within the next 25 years it is likely that soldiers will wear helmets with a **head-up display** capable of showing maps, pictures and video images, for instance from thermal-imaging cameras (cameras that detect heat). Advanced helmets will be linked to the **GPS** system, to show the location of friendly and enemy troops. The main block to such a helmet at present is the lack of a lightweight and durable power supply.

Body armour

Soldiers wear body armour to protect themselves from injury, and for future soldiers this is likely to be improved. Body armour has to stop the forward motion of a bullet or flying **shrapnel** and disperse the object's energy within a centimetre or so (before it reaches the skin of the wearer).

Currently, there are two forms of body armour: hard and soft. Hard body armour is made from ceramic or metal plates. It gives excellent protection, but it is bulky and heavy and can be awkward and tiring to wear.

Soft body armour is generally more comfortable, but it does not give the same level of protection. It is made from a material called Kevlar, which is incredibly strong but light. The Kevlar is woven into a mesh. When a projectile hits the mesh, it pulls on the interlaced strands and spreads the energy over a wide area. This is similar to what happens when a football hits a goal net. The strands that form the armour must only stretch so far, so the weave of the fibres is very tight.

Bullet-proof vests are basically soft armour, although it is possible to add hard armour plates over the top. Vests are made of many layers of strong, tightly woven fibres sandwiched between layers of plastic film, and the whole thing is encased in a protective outer cover.

A young British soldier, undergoing Pre-Commando training, with a display of all his personal equipment. Any equipment for a special task would be added to this kit!

A heavy load

Today's foot soldier is required to carry large quantities of equipment – weapons, ammunition, flak jacket and other clothing, food and water, night-vision aids and communications. In the future, the amount of equipment is likely to increase. Even though advances such as the multi-layered uniform (see page 47) will cut down on equipment weight, soldiers will probably still have a lot to carry.

Exoskeletons

So what if a soldier could be made stronger? In the future, it is possible that soldiers could wear an outer covering – a sort of hard shell like the exoskeleton of an insect, powered by mechanical muscles. This would enable soldiers to run and jump faster and further, and to carry heavy loads for long distances.

Soldiers of the future might look rather like medieval knights in armour. These knights wore such heavy armour that they had to be winched on to their horses. The armour of future soldiers will be made of materials that are much lighter, and motors would improve their strength to make them many times more agile and powerful. Extra strength would allow the soldier to carry additional weapon systems and **sensors**, which would probably be built into the exoskeleton.

Any exoskeleton would have to be strong and flexible, and be capable of protecting itself and the wearer. It is likely that it would be made from advanced **composites**. The motors that power the skeleton would need a lightweight and compact power source that could supply power for at least 24 hours without recharging.

Staying alert

Soldiers can have the best equipment possible, but one problem that cannot be overcome with technology is soldier fatigue. During an **offensive**, soldiers may be active for long periods of time and they have to stay alert. Important decisions may have to be made after many hours of activity.

To overcome fatigue, soldiers learn to grab short periods of sleep when the opportunity presents itself. This may be during the day rather than at night, and this disrupts their regular sleep pattern. Everyone sleeps less well during daylight hours, partly because of the light and the noise level and partly because of the influence of their own 'body clock' telling them that they should be awake. Mealtimes, too, are altered. Soldiers may suffer from digestive disorders, because of irregular meal times and the fact that meals may be hurried. All these changes can reduce mental alertness and make mistakes more likely.

Soldiers can be prepared to deal with fatigue. During army training sessions they are subjected to battlefield conditions so that they experience the problems of fatigue before being in a real combat situation. Sometimes soldiers can take drugs to increase their level of alertness temporarily. In the future, new drugs may be developed to help protect soldiers and keep them fit and effective. However, the body cannot keep working without rest indefinitely, so military planners must take soldier fatigue into account.

Future battlefield

It is certain that the army of tomorrow will look quite different to that operating today. In the future, the military will be more mobile and able to react more quickly to world events. Armed forces will be able to strike more accurately and with great precision.

In futuristic films, such as *Terminator*, there are cyberwars in which robots do the killing without direct command by humans. In the future, there will undoubtedly be more robot vehicles and other automated equipment. Artificial **intelligence** could enable computers to process the data and make decisions.

War on the street

Soldiers may be equipped with enhanced equipment designed to deal with the urban environment. For example, they may have an 'anti-sniper system' – a portable computer that can work out the trajectory (path) of a bullet and follow it back to pinpoint the exact location of an enemy sniper. **Non-lethal weapons** will be an important part of the urban soldier's armoury, for use in situations such as crowd control.

Hypersonic UAVs

Currently, long-range bombing missions can take up to 44 hours to complete. They may involve multiple air-to-air refuelling procedures, and often have to rely on airbases in other countries. As part of the new strategy to have a more mobile armed force, the USA is developing a **hypersonic** unmanned aerial vehicle (UAV) that is capable of attacking anywhere on Earth within two hours. The program is called Falcon, and it is planned to be operational by 2025. Falcon is a remote-controlled aircraft capable of taking off from a conventional runway. It can fly in the upper atmosphere at more than five times the speed of sound and deliver six tonnes of precision-guided bombs or missiles on targets up to 14,000 kilometres away.

Falcon will be powered by a type of engine known as a scramjet. Conventional jet engines work by drawing in air, compressing it, mixing it with fuel and then exploding it in

When it comes into use, the hypersonic vehicle, Falcon, could be virtually invulnerable. No other fighter aircraft or anti-aircraft missile could fly as high or as fast.

a combustion chamber. The exhaust gases from the explosion provide the **thrust** that drives the aircraft along. A scramjet only begins to work at speeds of about 5000 km/h. At these speeds air is forced into the engine at supersonic speeds as the aircraft moves along. Fuel is mixed with this **supersonic** air and exploded to produce thrust. The scramjet will take the Falcon up to a top speed of nearly 9000 km/h.

Space warfare

Many of the latest advances in weapons and systems (for example **GPS**) depend on **satellites** for their operation. In future, it is possible that weapons systems will be placed in orbit around the Earth, and that future battles will be won by the country that dominates space. Of course, as soon as one country puts a weapon platform into space, others would feel the need to defend against that by deploying anti-satellite missiles, or even satellites designed to find and destroy orbiting weapons platforms.

Fortunately, space has remained relatively 'unmilitary' to date. Those military satellites that are in space today are almost all concerned with communications, navigation or **surveillance**. However, this could change in the future

Microbots

Military forces already use robots for dangerous tasks that need to be done at long range without risk to humans, such as bomb disposal and surveillance. Most of the robots in use today are relatively large and limited in the applications for which they can be used. However scientists are developing tiny ground-based robots that will be just five centimetres long. They are called **smart** microbots and they will be able to carry out a range of tasks, from surveillance and detecting minefields on the battlefield to checking for suspected **terrorist** booby traps. Microbots have the added bonus that several of them can work together to perform tasks that would be beyond the ability of a single, complex robot.

Microbots are made from smart materials and make use of new forms of energy storage. Since a microbot is similar in size and mass to an insect, scientists have turned to biology to solve the problems of movement. Each microbot consists of a single silicon chip and a number of 'legs'. Depending on the design, the microbot can walk, jump, climb, crawl or slither.

Robotic insects

Scientists are also developing a range of robot aircraft known as micro air vehicles (MAVs). They will be far smaller than any conventional UAV. They will be able to operate on their own, buzzing over enemy territory and sending back information. Aircraft of this size (about 15 centimetres) would be too small to be noticed.

One prototype, called an Entomopter, is based on the design of an insect. Its 'body' contains the power source and the fuel tank. There are two pairs of wings, with a span of 15 centimetres. The wings are made from thin film supported by stiff yet flexible 'veins'. Entomopter even has legs that provide extra fuel storage and help to control movement in the air.

The power source for the Entomopter is a 'chemical muscle'. As well as powering the wings, the chemical muscle also provides a small amount of electricity to run **sensors** and communications systems. Waste gas produced by the chemical muscle is used to steer the tiny robot through the air and to run Entomopter's navigation system. One possible use of Entomopter is in the exploration of Mars. It could be used as a scout vehicle to check out the terrain for a robot rover.

Smart dust

The development of a miniature sensor the size of a grain of rice could become a powerful tool for gathering information about enemy movements. Such sensors, known as 'motes', will be self-powered, undetectable, cheap and very simple to use. Prototype motes about the size of a matchbox already exist, but future generations of mote will be small enough to float safely to the ground if dropped from an aircraft.

Motes will be intelligent and will take energy directly from their environment, probably from movement or sunlight. Different motes could be used to monitor almost anything from temperature to vibration, noise and even gravity. Each mote would be part of a network, communicating with a few near neighbours.

Each mote will have an on-board computer. It spends 99 per cent of its time asleep, so power requirements are tiny – just one thousandth of the power used by a mobile phone. Each mote processes the data from its sensor and transmits the processed information to the surrounding motes. The information is passed along the network to a control station. If one mote fails, the others reconfigure.

E-bombs

When a nuclear bomb explodes, it gives off a powerful burst of radio waves that destroys electronic systems. Non-nuclear weapons that produce a similar pulse, strong enough to damage electronic systems, are now being developed. It is likely that such 'E- bombs' will be fitted in **cruise missiles** in the near future.

The E-Bomb emits a very brief, high-power burst of a few microseconds in length. The energy produced can enter an electronic or electrical system through an antenna or unshielded wiring, and damage electronic components even when they are not operating. Anything electrical is at risk, including **radar** systems, radios, GPS receivers and computers.

The E-bombs under development by the military are sophisticated weapons, but a basic weapon could be built cheaply using simple components. This could make E-bombs attractive to terrorists who could cause considerable damage by setting off an E-bomb over a city, especially a financial centre such as London or New York. The bomb could effectively 'fry' everything electric and electronic within several kilometres of the point of detonation. However, the damage would not stop with the initial pulse. Over the next 15 minutes or so, collapsing electrical systems and communications grids would create their own smaller pulses, rather like the aftershocks that follow an earthquake.

'These weapons are designed almost exclusively for destroying electronic systems. They minimize collateral damage [unnecessary, non-target damage], over-killing and wasted effort. I tend to think this could make war more humane. So, such weapons are very attractive to governments that do not wish to be seen to use "disproportionate force".'

Loren Thompson, author of a recent study on
directed-energy weapons

Genetic weapons

The Human Genome Project has worked out the sequence of human **DNA** and identified thousands of genes. As the functions of more and more genes are discovered, it becomes increasingly likely that genes will be used to develop new **weapons of mass destruction**. The British Medical Association (BMA) has warned that such knowledge could be used to create 'race-specific' genetic weapons, designed to affect only particular ethnic groups. Such a weapon is a frightening thought and it will be vital that future governments ensure that information about the genome is never misused.

A much more likely genetic weapon is the use of **genetic engineering** to target agricultural crops. Already crop plants have been modified so that they are resistant to disease or weed-killers. In the future, crop plants could be altered so that they failed to grow properly, or so that the crop contained poisons. The world's seed stocks could become contaminated with such modified seed meaning that populations could starve or become poisoned. This could lead to widespread hunger and even whole populations being poisoned by the food that they eat.

Concluding thoughts

Modern armies are now increasingly involved in peacekeeping, fighting against **guerilla forces** and combatting terrorism. Today's armed forces are also far more 'thinly spread' than in the past. British military forces, for instance, are deployed in more than 80 countries around the world. This is very different to 30 years ago, when the bulk of the forces were concentrated in Europe. This means that the armed forces have to be mobile and able to react quickly to world events.

Both the UK and USA have announced that their military forces are to be reorganized into smaller, lighter units that can be dispatched anywhere in the world at a moment's notice. There will be a greater emphasis on the role of special forces on the ground, such as the British SAS and the US Green Berets, while the air force will be armed with more precision-guided **smart** bombs and the navy with more **cruise missiles**.

A British soldier mixes with local children in Iraq while carrying out peace-keeping duties.

It is likely that the threat of chemical and biological weapons will remain. **Terrorists** may be tempted to use them because of the psychological damage that they can inflict. Another future possibility might be the use of **genetic engineering** as a form of **WMD**.

With modern technology, warfare can now be monitored and controlled remotely. Here, controllers in the Combined Air Operations Center are monitoring on-going missions during the Iraq War from an air base on the Arabian Peninsula.

War at a distance

Warfare is becoming less personal and more remote. Many of tomorrow's soldiers may not even see the enemy. The number of soldiers involved in action is generally lower than in the past. For example, the pinpoint accuracy of precision-guided missiles used to wipe out key installations during the Iraq war in 2003 meant that fewer troops were needed to win the war. However, this technological advantage proved to be of little or no use in 'winning the peace'. When the role of the military changed to peacekeeping rather than all-out war, more soldiers were needed on the ground to keep order and to help rebuild the damaged country.

So will wars of the future be any quicker, easier or more humane than wars have been in the past? On the one hand, the increased use of robots and automated smart weapons means that fighting can be done from afar, saving the lives of soldiers. On the other, the rise in terrorism and **guerrilla warfare** means that, increasingly, the role of the military is to protect civilian populations against small groups that might attack in any situation. Training armed forces to deal with both these types of future war is a difficult task.

'Another type of war, new in its intensity, ancient in its origin – war by guerrillas … war by ambush instead of by combat; by infiltration instead of aggression, seeking victory by eroding and exhausting the enemy instead of engaging him.'

US President John F Kennedy in the 1960s, talking to graduates of West Point Military Academy

Timeline

1925   Nations sign Geneva Protocol prohibiting the use of **toxic** gases and bacteriological methods in warfare. However, the Protocol is ignored by some nations, such as Italy, which used mustard gas against Abyssinian troops in a war in 1935–36.

1939   World War II starts.

1942   Testing of anthrax on Gruinard Island, Scotland renders the island uninhabitable for 48 years.

1944   A form of **cruise missile**, the V-1 or 'buzz bomb', is developed by Nazi Germany.

1945   First nuclear bomb, code-named Trinity, is exploded as a test on 16 July in New Mexico, USA. On the 6th August, a **fission** bomb called Little Boy is detonated over Hiroshima, Japan.

1949   North Atlantic Treaty Organization is established, comprising ten European and two North American countries.

1952   World's first hydrogen **fusion** bomb is test-detonated on Elugelap Island in the Pacific.

1964   The USA more directly enters war with North Vietnam after two US destroyers are fired upon by a North Vietnamese torpedo boat. The USA and the forces of its allies (including Australia) try to fight a **conventional war** but the North Vietnamese use **guerrilla** tactics. The USA uses chemical warfare to destroy the forests that are hiding enemy troops.

1968   Troubles in Northern Ireland start. IRA uses **terrorist** tactics to try to end British rule in Northern Ireland.

1975   South Vietnam is invaded by North Vietnamese troops and remaining US troops forced to withdraw.

         Signing of the Convention on the Prohibition of the Development, Production and Stockpiling of Bacteriological and Toxin Weapons.

1979   Soviet forces invade Afghanistan. They are met with resistance from guerrilla fighters who successfully overcome the greater strength of the Soviet forces.

1982   Falklands War starts when Argentinian forces take over the British Falkland Islands.

1984 IRA bomb a Brighton hotel in an attempt to kill members of the British Conservative government during a political party conference.

1985 Nuclear Non-Proliferation Treaty is signed on 1 July by the USA, UK and Soviet Union and 59 other countries. It is not signed by China or France.

1989 US air force's B2 Spirit **stealth** bomber flies for the first time.

1991 Operation Desert Storm (Gulf War) begins on 16 January. A **coalition** of allied forces, led by the USA, launches a war against Iraq after Iraqi troops invade Kuwait.

1993 Chemical Weapons Convention is established. This is a multinational agreement to eliminate production and storage of chemical weapons.

1995 Terrorists carry out Sarin attack on the Tokyo subway in Japan.

1996 International community draws up the Comprehensive Test Ban Treaty which bans all forms of nuclear explosion.

1999 The Ottawa Convention, a treaty that bans the use of anti-personnel mines, comes into effect.

A blackout bomb, released by a Nighthawk stealth fighter, is used for the first time as part of NATO strikes against Serbia.

2001 On 11 September, terrorists fly two planes into the twin towers of the World Trade Center in New York, causing their collapse and the death of thousands of people.

US Senator Tom Daschle receives a letter containing anthrax spores. The spores infect 25 people. Offices are closed and parts of the US Mail shut down.

2002 A single 900-kg **thermobaric** bomb is used for the first time in combat against fighters hiding in cave complexes in Afghanistan

Outbreaks of SARS in China.

Russian troops use chemical agent to subdue Chechen fighters holding hundreds of people hostage in Moscow theatre.

North Korea admits to having a nuclear weapons programme despite signing a treaty agreeing to abandon this.

2003 Iraq War starts on 20 March.

Glossary

adaptive material material that changes shape if exposed to heat, electricity or electromagnetism

antibiotic type of drug that kills or inhibits the growth of harmful bacteria, for example penicillin

artillery heavy guns firing explosive shells and launchers firing missiles

atoms smallest particles in an element that can take part in a chemical reaction

ceramic any material that is first shaped and then hardened by means of heat

coalition temporary alliance of countries to fight a war

composite material in which fibres of one material are embedded in another material in order to make a stronger substance

conventional war war in which two opposing armies meet and fight each other using large numbers of soldiers, tanks, armoured vehicles and aircraft

cruise missile guided missile that uses a lifting wing and a jet propulsion system to allow sustained flight. Generally designed to carry a large conventional or nuclear warhead many hundreds of kilometres.

deoxyribonucleic acid (DNA) type of nucleic acid found in the nucleus of a cell, which carries the genetic information

depleted uranium (DU) by-product of the nuclear industry used in armour-piercing ammunition

enriched uranium uranium that has been processed so that it can be used as fuel for a nuclear reactor or in nuclear weapons

fermenter device for growing microbes under controlled conditions, often on a large scale

fuel cell device similar to a battery in which oxygen and hydrogen are reacted together to produce electricity

genetic engineering process by which the DNA (genetic make up) of an organism is altered by scientists. This can be achieved by inserting a gene taken from another organism or by removing a gene.

global positioning system (GPS) system of satellites which send digital signals to Earth that are picked up by receivers and used to determine location

guerrilla forces member of an independent or irregular fighting force, often motivated for political reasons

head-up display display in which information is projected into the line of sight of the wearer

hijacking illegally seizing control of a vehicle

hypersonic speeds more than five times the speed of sound, known as Mach 5+

immune system body's natural defence system, which protects it against infection by disease-causing organisms

incubation period period between becoming infected with a disease and showing any symptoms

inertial navigation system navigation system that works out its position by knowing its initial speed and direction of travel, then uses sensors to detect changes in its speed or direction

intelligence information about the enemy

jamming blocking enemy communications with, interferences that make a signal unintelligible

laser instrument that generates an intense beam of light of a specific wavelength and which is used in guidance systems of missiles

nanometre one billionth of a metre or one millionth of a millimetre

nerve agent chemical that interferes with the normal functioning of the nervous system, often by blocking the passage of nerve impulses along neurones

neutron uncharged particle found in the nucleus of an atom

non-lethal weapon weapon that stuns or incapacitates a person, but does not kill

nuclear fission splitting the nucleus of an atom into smaller fragments

nuclear fusion joining two small atoms together to form one larger atom

offensive in military terms, a large-scale attack

pathogen organism that causes disease

plutonium dense radioactive metallic element used in some weapons

radar instrument used for detecting the direction, range or presence of aircraft, ships and other objects which sends out pulses of high frequency electromagnetic waves

radiation emission of energy as electromagnetic waves

radioactive giving off radiation, caused by the spontaneous splitting of atomic nuclei and the emission of small particles

radioactive fallout cloud of radioactive particles of dust and debris that falls backs to the ground following a nuclear explosion

satellite artificial body, placed in orbit around the Earth that sends and receives signals

sensor device which is designed to detect or measure certain properties such as magnetism, temperature and pressure and emit a signal

shrapnel fragments of metal from a bullet or bomb

simulation computer model of a process

smart computer guided or electronically controlled

stealth something that has been designed to be hard for radar and infrared sensors to detect

supersonic greater than the speed of sound

superstructure upper part of a ship, above the hull

surveillance watching a person or an area closely

terrorist a person who uses violence to achieve their political aims while disguised as a civilian

thermobaric producing heat and pressure

thrust force that pushes an object forwards

toxin poison produced by a living organism such as a bacterium

United Nations intergovernmental organisation, founded in 1945, concerned with international peace and security

vaccine substance that stimulates the body's defences to give immunity against a particular disease

weapon of mass destruction (WMD) weapon which is either nuclear, biological or chemical and which is designed to attack large numbers of people or property

Sources of information

Websites

The following websites give information on all aspects of hi-tech warfare:

http://www.nuclearfiles.org
Website of the Nuclear Age Peace Foundation with information concerning nuclear energy and weapons. This site is an educational resource exploring the political, legal and ethical challenges stemming from the continued existence of nuclear weapons.

http://science.howstuffworks.com
Website of the Federation of American Scientists with good explanations of all sorts of topics including scientific technology and military weaponry.

www.fas.org
Website with good scientific resources, not just those concerned with biological, chemical and nuclear weapons.

www.stimson.org
Website of the Henry L Stimson Center, Chemical Weapons History and Controls.

http://www.cbiac.apgea.army.mil/
Website of the Chemical and Biological Defence Information Analysis Center.

http://www.dodccrp.org/steinncw.htm
Website on Network Centric Warfare.

http://www.cdi.org/
Website containing defence information.

Author sources

In addition to the websites above, the author used the following materials in the writing of this book:

The Physical World, Ken Dobson (Nelson Balanced Science, 1991)

Magazines – *New Scientist, Focus, Science*

Index